American Art Association

Modern Paintings

The Private Collection of Abraham Disbecker

American Art Association

Modern Paintings
The Private Collection of Abraham Disbecker

ISBN/EAN: 9783744642279

Printed in Europe, USA, Canada, Australia, Japan

Cover: Foto ©Thomas Meinert / pixelio.de

More available books at **www.hansebooks.com**

CATALOGUE

SALE, FRIDAY, APRIL 1st

AT THE AMERICAN ART GALLERIES

BEGINNING AT 8:30 O'CLOCK, P.M.

SCHEFFER (A.).

No. 1. The Consultation.

A small canvas showing two men seated, talking together. The costumes are of the period of François Premier and the color is rich and full.

Height, 8¼ inches. Width, 6¼ inches.

Signed at the left.

MUÑOZ (DOMINGO).

Born in Spain. Contemporary. A celebrated genre painter, whose work is marked by fine color qualities and refined and accurate drawing.

No. 2. The Spanish Admiral.

Small panel, showing the head and bust of an elderly man, with a keen face, the expression denoting a somewhat peppery character, and the head capped with a high cocked hat, trimmed with fur and a scarlet cockade. A high scarlet collar, scarlet facings on the blue coat, and a broad white sword-belt, with two narrow crimson stripes at the edges, complete the costume. A delicately painted characterization in the clever manner of the Spanish-Roman style.

Height, 11 inches. Length, 14 inches.
Signed at the right.

MIRALLES (E.).

Contemporary painter of the French School, whose pictures are generally of figures out of doors. His works are noted for their good drawing and attractive color.

No. 3. In the Fields.

A man in hunting costume of the time of Louis XIII, holds in leash a dog, whose action shows that he sees game and wishes to spring forward. The man, a stalwart well-drawn figure, holds him back, and the environment presents a pleasant landscape on a summer day. A very cleverly executed little picture, full of life and movement.

Height, 9¼ inches. Width, 7¼ inches.

Signed at the ——

LAUGÉE (GEORGES).

Born at Montivilliers (Seine-Inferieure), France.
Contemporary. Pupil of his father, D. F. Laugée,
and of Pils and Lehmann. Medal at the Paris Universal Exposition, 1889; a regular exhibitor at the
Salon, and a well known painter of peasant life.

No. 4. Breakfast in the Meadow.

With her back against the trunk of a big tree,
that grows in a meadow where there are haycocks
in the middle distance and cool shadow in the
foreground, a peasant girl is seated eating "la
soupe." It is her mid-day lunch taken long after
the first breakfast at the beginning of the day's
work, and the rest and food are grateful. By her
side is a great loaf of home-made bread, and a bottle of cider. In her pink bodice, dark skirt, and
blue apron, this comely worker in the fields presents an attractive picture. The landscape is com-
petently treated and agreeable in its color scheme.
The interpretation of the episode is picturesque
and veracious.

Height, 18 inches. Length, 22 inches.
Signed at the right. Dated 1887.

WAGNER (FERDINAND).

Born at Passau, January 25, 1847. Pupil of Munich Academy and of Quaglio. Visited Rome, and in 1876, Venice. A noted artist of the German School, and famous for his coloring.

No. 5. Flowers.

A striking composition of masses of light and dark, with rich effective color. A large bunch of pink, red, yellow, and white roses naturally arranged, with a profusion of glowing tints, and a tall vase on the left containing three pale roses of delicate hue. The roses are large and in luxuriant bloom, and the juxtaposition of the brilliant colors artistically managed with the fine drawing make of this picture a handsome decorative picture.

Height, 30 inches. Width, 21½ inches.
Signed at the left.

LAUGÉE (DESIRÉ FRANÇOIS).

No. 6. The Gossips.

The scene is in a wheat-field, on a fine day, when the sky is blue, with clouds of white and gray. Two women, who have been gleaning, are talking while one, who is sitting on a sheaf, cuts a loaf of bread, and the other, standing near at hand, holds two sheaves in her hands. The standing shocks of grain, and the other elements of the landscape, harmonize with the figures in composition and color, and the picture bears a true pastoral aspect.

Height, 15 inches.   Length, 18 inches.
Signed at the right.

DUPRÉ (JULIEN).

Born in Paris, March 17, 1851. Pupil of Pils and Lehman at the École des Beaux-Arts, and of D. F. Laugée. Silver medal, Paris Universal Exposition, 1889. Chevalier of the Legion of Honor. Paints figures and landscape, and is a strong cattle painter. His style is original, and his work is of high technical excellence.

No. 7. Normandy Peasant.

A figure of a girl in blue and purple woolen garments, and with a red 'kerchief on her head, coming through the fields. The sky is gray, and the upper part of the figure is relieved against it with fine effect ; a pitchfork and rake, which she carries over her left shoulder, appearing with picturesque lines in silhouette. On her right arm she carries a large square lunch basket or kit, in which the noon-day meal for the workers in the field is taken to them. A frankly painted work by a painter whose life-work has been the study of the peasant and his picturesque surroundings.

Height, 13¼ inches. Width, 9 inches.
Signed at the left. Dated 1886.

GRISON (JULES ADOLPHE).

Born at Bordeaux. Pupil of Lequien. A regular exhibitor at the Salon, and the recipient of various artistic honors.

No. 8. Jean Jacques Rousseau aux Charmettes.

This beautiful little picture shows the great Rousseau in a morning gown and a fur-bordered cap, looking out of his window at The Charmettes on the garden and forest surrounding his sylvan retreat. The figure is a portrait and an excellent one, and the picture was painted by Grison *sur place* in the room occupied by Rousseau, for the painter lives a good part of the time at Thonex, near Geneva. This picture, like all the Grisons in the collection, was purchased by Mr. Disbecker directly from the artist. The room shows a table, a wall case of books, and inside shutters turned back from the open window. Rousseau holds in his hand a quill pen, and the head, no larger than a dime, is painted with admirable art. Both in its historical aspect and by reason of the astonishingly clever painting of the figure and accessories, this is a very remarkable work.

Height, 7¼ inches. Width, 5¼ inches.

Signed at the left.

JACQUET (JEAN GUSTAVE).

Born in Paris, May 25, 1846. Pupil of Bouguereau. First class medal, Paris Salon, 1875. Chevalier of the Legion of Honor. His portraits and pictures of women have given him a high reputation as a painter whose work is marked by delicacy of color and charm of expression.

No. 9. Delphine.

A head of a lovely girl with dark hair and eyes, with a white ruff about her neck, and a blue and plum-colored corsage. This charming head is an artistic and not a commercial example of the talent of a gifted painter of beautiful women, and the expression is evidently studied for its inherent grace and charm. Painted with full modelling and refined and subtile color.

Height, 12¼ inches. Width, 9¼ inches.
Signed at the upper right.

RAFFAËLLI (JEAN FRANÇOIS).

Born in Paris. Contemporary. Gold medal Paris Universal Exposition, 1889. Chevalier of the Legion of Honor. He made his *début* as an artist at the first exhibition of the " Independents," or " Impressionists " in Paris, in 1879, and has since then achieved solid success, and is rated as one of the most individual of modern painters. His works are especially remarkable for the study of character in modern types.

No. 10. His Morning Exercise.

One of the interesting character pictures which have made the name of the painter known to the art world in both hemispheres. An old man with a gray beard sits on a bench under the trees by the river side with his walking-stick and newspaper. Something has attracted his attention, and he looks up with his spectacles on his nose, his expression showing interest and *bonhomie*. Across the stream is seen a country inn embowered among the trees, with an arbor before the doorway. The picture is painted with the characteristic Raffaëlli handling, and shows the delicate harmonies of gray, white, green, and black, which are favorite notes in the artist's color schemes. It is individual in style and personal in execution.

Height, 18¼ inches. Width, 12¼ inches.
Signed at the right.

RICO (MARTIN).

Born at Madrid. Pupil of Féderico de Madrazo and afterwards studied in Paris and Rome. Various medals at Paris Salon and Universal Expositions. Chevalier of the Legion of Honor.

No. 11. Garden of San Silvestre, Venice.

The water of the canal fills the immediate foreground, and at the gate in the wall, through which may be seen the trees and flowers of the garden, stands a young woman with a red shawl about her shoulders. To the right is a gondola, with a man playing a guitar in a mid-day serenade, and above the garden wall and trees rises a house with warm, white stucco, and the tower of the church. Over all is the bright blue sky. This picture bears the characteristic marks in handling and general treatment that make Rico's pictures of Venice so distinctive, and in composition and subject it is extremely attractive.

Height, 19½ inches. Width, 11½ inches.
Signed at the left.

MONCHABLON (F. JAN).

Born in France. A contemporary painter of landscape whose works, which he began to exhibit only a few years since, have brought him a remarkable reputation. Belongs to a family of artists whose home is in the Vosges, and is not to be confused with Xavier Monchablon, the classical painter. His pictures are wonderfully truthful in detail and equally remarkable for breadth of general effect.

No. 12. A Quiet Corner.

This picture in gray weather is different in motive from the wide stretches of country the artist usually takes for his themes. There are fields and gardens behind a village with stone walls dividing the small holdings of the inhabitants, cows pasturing here and there, and a woman in a dress of black and white watching them. A big willow tree with its heavy topped trunk appears at the left, its delicately foliaged branches spreading upward against the sky. Detail is united with breadth, and the scene breathes a pastoral air justifying the title.

Height, 13½ inches. Width, 10½ inches.
Signed at the right. Dated 1889.

DAUBIGNY (KARL).

Born in Paris, June 9, 1846. Son and pupil of Charles François Daubigny. Formed a style of his own and received medals at the Salon. His landscapes are highly appreciated in France, but are not very well known in the United States. Died in Paris in 1886.

No. 13. Landscape.

Gray and pearly in general effect of color, this landscape by Karl Daubigny might easily be taken for a work by his father, the great landscape master. But it contains also distinctive personal qualities such as mark the productions of Karl Daubigny, who, in a comparatively short career, achieved a decided individual success as a faithful and artistic portrayer of nature. The simple elements of the composition, the river, the trees in the middle distance, the women washing on the shore, and the gray sky with dark clouds in the upper portion, are painted broadly, frankly, and with great truth of observation.

Height, 9½ inches. Length, 15½ inches. Signed at the left. Dated 1885.

BERNE-BELLECOUR (ÉTIENNE-PROSPER).

Born at Boulogne, June 29, 1838. Pupil of Picot and Barrias. Chevalier of the Legion of Honor; medals at the Salon and Universal Expositions. The painter of many excellent works depicting the soldier's life, which have given him an enviable reputation.

No. 14. Le Premier Déjeûner.

Two French troopers, their red and blue uniforms covered by long gray riding cloaks, are sitting on the ground, leaning against bunches of faggots, which they have been to the forest to procure in the early morning, while a third stands nearby cutting a loaf. A big brown dog sits beside the latter and expectantly waits for his share of the frugal repast. The soldiers have stopped by the roadside on the way to the barracks in the town, which appears in the background, and the scene is a most picturesque illustration of the soldier's life. The composition is excellent, and the general aspect of the picture, with the stalwart figures of the troopers and the gray-day effect of the landscape, is extremely attractive. Unlike de Neuville, Berne-Bellecour seldom paints soldiers in action, or battle scenes, but finds his subjects principally in the daily life of the troops, in barracks, or on the march during manœuvres. This picture is a fine example of his artistic treatment of one of his favorite themes.

Height, 18 inches. Length, 24 inches. Signed at the right.

DEMONT (ADRIEN-LOUIS).

Born at Douai, France. Contemporary landscape painter. Pupil of Emile Breton, son-in-law of Jules Breton, being the husband of the celebrated painter Madame Virginie Demont Breton. Chevalier of the Legion of Honor; Gold Medal, Paris Universal Exposition, 1889. His picture, " A Mill," is in the Luxembourg Museum, Paris, and his works are considered as among the best of modern landscapes. Excels in moonlight effects.

No. 15. Moonlight at Montgeron.

This is a beautiful effect on the long twilight of Northern France. A road leads into the picture, passing through the meadows with a tree on the right of it, about in the middle of the composition, and there are hills and foliage beyond. The picture is full of air, and the evening atmosphere is delightfully depicted. Form is observed in every part of the picture without detracting from the mysterious evening effect, and the color is truthful in its reserved, full power. The moon rising above the horizon shines softly over the landscape, and the general aspect of the picture is exceedingly poetical.

Height, 18 inches. Length, 31¼ inches. Signed at the right.

MONCHABLON (F. JAN).

No. 16. Le Premier Soleil.

Over the wide stretch of flat fields, partly plowed in the foreground, browse a few sheep. In the middle distance is a long low line of red-roofed houses and barns. Beyond is a vast expanse of country with hills and valleys. A fine sky of the most delicate tints, exquisitely gradated from the lightest part on the right, near where the sun is, to the bluest portions on the left, further away from it, fills the upper part of the picture, and the air of springtime is apparent in every part of the work. - Monchablon might be called the Meissonier of landscape, for his handling of detail, as in this picture, is marvellous ; but he also paints with so much breadth of conception that his pictures are complete in the large sense. This is a notable example of his talent.

Height, 20 inches. Length, 29 inches.
Signed at the right. Dated 1879.

CORTAZZO (ORESTE).

Born in Italy. Contemporary. A celebrated genre painter whose works are in several known collections in the United States.

No. 17. The Interrupted Sitting.

In a studio, filled with rich properties, rugs, tapestries, furniture, armor, stuffs, and costumes, an artist is shown, who has just risen from his easel, where he has been painting a nude figure, to welcome two ladies, who have come to make a visit. The foremost of the two is young and aristocratic looking, and is dressed in a costume of rose-color with a black lace mantilla. The other lady, who follows her, is of noble aspect, and a footman appears behind her, who has just drawn apart the curtains that shield the entrance doorway. In the meantime the model has fled to a refuge behind a screen at the left of the picture, where she stands wrapped in a red covering, and must wait till the interview is over. The figures and accessories are painted skillfully, and the picture is bright in its color scheme, and effective in composition.

Height, 18 inches. Length, 27 inches.
Signed at the right. Dated 1870.

LAUGÉE (DESIRE FRANÇOIS).

Born at Maromme (Seine-Inferieure), France, January 25, 1823. Father of Georges Laugée. Pupil of Picot. Chevalier of the Legion of Honor ; first class medal, Salon of 1861. Member of the Institute of France. He first painted portraits, but afterward turned to out-of-doors genre, and his reputation was made chiefly in the latter class of works.

No. 18. After the Rain.

A white walled cottage on the left of the picture stands on a village street with a bit of its thatched roof showing at the upper part of the canvas. At the door in the foreground on the stone stoop is a peasant girl with two pails of water, turning her head to speak to another woman at the farther end of the house, who dips up water from a tub placed under the rain spout. Green grass on the sidewalk, dark trees at the end of the street, a rain-washed gray sky, and excellent atmospheric effect combine to set off the principal figure with pleasing effect. The picture shows skillful handiwork and much truth of observation, and the figure of the girl with her picturesque costume is pretty and attractive.

Height, 18 inches. Width, 15 inches.
Signed at the right.

MONCHABLON (F. JAN).

No. 19. Un Chemin dans les Moissons.

Under a beautiful blue sky, with clouds of white
near the horizon burnt out by the heat of a summer's day, yet massive enough to show their forma-
tion, lie wide fields of ripe grain with a road
leading through them to a valley beyond and
continuing in a white strip over the next hill.
The vast expanse of country is covered with
crops ripening in the sunshine even to the distant
hills at the horizon. In the road in the middle
distance, a peasant with his scythe over his
shoulder is seen walking along with his sweetheart, his arm around her waist. There is a fine
sense of atmosphere in the picture, and the tender
blue sky is gradated in color with the most
wonderful delicacy. This feature of the landscape painting of Monchablon, always so remarkable, is here exhibited in one of its most beautiful
phases, and the picture is amazingly true to nature
and poetic as well.

Height, 19½ inches. Length, 25½ inches.
Signed at the right.

23

LAUGÉE (GEORGES).

No. 20.   The Gleaners.

A pretty pastoral showing a peasant girl standing in a wheat-field with her arms akimbo, with a
lad before her on his knees binding her sheaf.
The figures are well characterized, the composition is agreeable in its lines, and the tone of the
landscape harmonizing with the colors of the
dress of the peasants, forms an attractive setting
for this poem of the fields.

Height, 21½ inches.   Length, 26½ inches.
Signed at the right.   Dated 1886.

MADRAZO (RAYMUNDO DE).

Born in Rome, July 24, 1841. Son and pupil of Don Féderico de Madrazo y Kunt, of the École des Beaux-Arts, and of Léon Cogniet, Paris. Gold Medal, Paris Universal Exposition, 1889 : Officer of the Legion of Honor. Several of his pictures were in the Wm. H. Stewart Collection, and he was the brother-in-law and a companion of Fortuny. He has resided in Paris during his artistic career, and is identified with the French School. At the present time (1898) he is in New York painting portraits.

No. 21. The Spanish Dance.

A scene in a beautiful garden with two young women in the picturesque costumes worn in Spain. One of the women, a dark gypsy-like creature, with black hair and a flower above her ear, clad in a gown of white with full, long skirt, and with a red shawl on her shoulders, dances with willowy grace to the music of a guitar played by her companion, a charming belle, slight, fair of complexion, with dark hair. She sits on a bench at the left of the picture before the high, white plastered garden wall, and wears a skirt of light, changeable blue and a shawl of yellow embroidered with flowers. Above the wall where vines are growing a bit of blue sky appears and a tree and a clump of bright blossoms make up the other elements of the composition. The picture is admirably painted throughout in Madrazo's best and most attractive style. It is delightful in sentiment, and remarkable for the grace of the

25

women ; and the exquisite execution of such parts as the hands of the seated figure is as accurate as Meissonier, yet as broad and suave as Velasquez.

Height, 25½ inches. Width, 16 inches.
Signed at the right.

ISABEY (ÉUGENE-LOUIS-GABRIEL).

Born in Paris, July 22, 1804 ; died there, April 26, 1886. Son and pupil of Jean Baptiste Isabey (1767–1855). In 1830 he accompanied the French Expedition to Algiers as royal marine painter. Officer of the Legion of Honor. Works in most of the State museums in France.

No. 22. Coast of Brittany.

An early work of sterling merit. A house and shipyard on shore to the left, the sea, with boats running before the wind, and a dramatic sky composed of storm clouds of black and gray, with the blue sky showing here and there make up the composition. The sea looks wide and threatening, and the color notes are so disposed as to make the general effect of the picture both striking and veracious. It is not unlike some of the celebrated Dutch marines in a general way, and as an example of the art of a man whose career was a continuous succession of triumphs, it is interesting in the extreme.

Height, 11 inches. Length, 17½ inches.
Signed at the left.

BOLDINI (GIOVANNI).

Born at Ferrara, Italy, in 1845. He first painted in Florence, but has resided in Paris and has been identified with the French school since 1872. At the present time (1898) he is passing the winter in New York, painting portraits. Boldini's earlier productions were small interiors, with figures and landscapes; these gained him great renown, and these pictures are eagerly sought for by collectors. For the past decade he has given his time to portrait painting, and in this branch of art has achieved an individual and commanding success. Chevalier of the Legion of Honor ; Grand Prize at the Paris Universal Exposition, 1889.

No. 23. On the Seine at Bougival.

A bright summer day at this suburban resort of holiday-making Parisians. Some steam launches and a paddle-wheel *bateau-mouche* are moored inshore at the left, and several rowboats, with their occupants in outing costume, are scattered about the river. A white house, with its walls and roof reflected in the water, stands on the bank, and the opposite bank shows trees and a towpath with a horse dragging his load. Birds are flying in the air, and the scene is full of gaiety. It is needless to say that everything is skillfully painted, and that the handling is of the cleverest, for this picture is one of those wonderfully clever works that made Boldini's high reputation.

Height, 11¼ inches. Length, 18½ inches. Signed at the left.

27

MONCHABLON (F. JAN).

No. 24. The Valley of the Saône.

A wheat-field in the foreground, with a wide stretch of country beyond. In a valley in the middle distance is a village with red roofs shining in the sun. The effect is in afternoon sunlight, with clouds hanging in the sky as they do on still, hot summer days. The sun is high up, and the landscape is bathed in its light, but with a somewhat misty gray effect of color. As in all of Monchablon's work, detail is given in this landscape with great accuracy and fidelity, but the general effect is exceedingly broad and unified. A characteristic scene in the beautiful country of the Côte-d'Or, and a remarkable example of the work of a painter whose rank as a *paysagiste* is deservedly high.

Height, 21 inches. Length, 29 inches.
Signed at the right. Dated 1887.

MURPHY (J. FRANCIS).

Born at Oswego, N. Y., in 1853. Self taught; National Academician; member of the American Water Color Society; Webb Prize, Society of American Artists, 1887. One of the best-known American landscape painters, whose works are in many private collections. They are highly appreciated for their refined color qualities and excellent composition.

No. 25. The Path to the Village.

A fine example of the work of one of the best-known American landscape painters. A narrow path winding through the grass leads over the crown of a slope, where the roofs of houses and a church tower appear. A vista of distant hills opens up the middle of the composition, and to the right there is a clump of trees. The composition is finely balanced, and the color shows the delicate greens and grays that the artist uses so successfully. Vigorously painted and unified in effect.

Height, 33½ inches. Width, 21 inches.

Signed at the right.

INNESS (GEORGE).

Born at Newburg, New York, May 1, 1825; died in Scotland, August 3, 1894, while on a summer journey. Pupil for a very short time of Regis Gignoux in New York, and visited Europe for study several times. National Academician, 1868. Generally recognized as the greatest of American landscape painters. His pictures, always founded on truth to nature, are remarkable for splendid color and wonderful atmospheric quality.

No. 26. Landscape.

A broad road at the outskirts of a village, with a flock of sheep coming toward the spectator, with a shepherd behind them. On the right there is a large spreading tree and clumps of foliage, a stone garden wall, a house half hidden in the verdure, and broad flat stretches of grass on either side of the road make a picturesque and peaceful ensemble. The sky in blue with white clouds in the horizon; and there are brilliant red notes here and there in the foliage—signs of the autumn. The color scheme is in general rich and warm, and the aspect of the picture is very attractive. A fine little specimen of the work of the great landscape painter.

Height, 12¼ inches. Length, 18 inches.
Signed at the left.

MAUVE (ANTON).

Born at Zaandam, Holland. Pupil of P. F. Van Os. Contemporary Dutch painter, whose pictures of sheep and landscape have a wide reputation, and are highly valued by connoisseurs. One of the leading artists in the modern Dutch school, and noted for his water color work as well as for his painting in oil.

No. 27. Shorn Sheep.

A small flock of sheep entering a barn, the door of which is held open by a peasant girl. With a weather-beaten gray barn, a sky of light gray, characteristic of the Holland climate, the pale greens of the landscape beyond, and the bare bodies of the sheep, one of which is black, the artist has carried out a fine scheme of sober tints, accenting it with a note of dark blue in the bonnet and skirt of the girl. The picture is fine in general tone, and the sheep are portrayed with the intimate knowledge that has made the painter famous. Always a favorite with American amateurs, Mauve in this example is seen in one of his best and most interesting phases.

Height, 17½ inches. Width, 15½ inches.
Signed at the right.

BONNAT (LÉON-JOSEPH-FLOREN-TIN).

Born at Bayonne in 1833. First studied in Madrid, where he was a pupil of Féderico de Madrazo, and afterwards was the favorite pupil of Léon Cogniet in Paris. M. Bonnat is the officially recognized head of the French school, and is a Member of the Institute. He received the medal of Honor at the Salon as long ago as 1869, and is a Commander of the Legion of Honor. Besides historical compositions and pictures of Italian peasant women and children he has painted a great number of famous portraits. The heads of royal houses, the presidents of the French Republic, great statesmen, men of letters, and fashionable ladies all sit for him in his grand studio in the Champs-Elysées.

No. 28. Italian Girl.

Half length picture of a pretty Italian peasant child. The upper part of the face is in shadow, and the olive complexion of the little girl, her dark eyes and hair contrast with the strong effect of light on the white head-dress and sleeves. An apron of red and dull yellow reaching up high on the bodice and red in the sleeves make attractive color notes. The expression is sweet and engaging. This is an excellent example of the great French master's small easel pictures which he now has no time to paint, and as such for its rarity, as well as for its fine quality as a *morceau*, is a very desirable picture.

Height, 14 inches. Width, 10¼ inches.
Signed at the upper left.

NEUVILLE (APHONSE MARIE DE).

Born at St. Omer (Pas-de-Calais), May 31, 1836 ; died in Paris, May 20, 1885.   Pupil of Picot.   He spent three years in the Law School in Paris, intending to be a barrister, but gave it up and became a painter, achieving early success.   Officer of the Legion of Honor.   The great battle painter of the Franco-Prussian War, and shares with Detaille the honor of being the foremost military painter of the century.

No. 29.   The Bivouac.

In this small picture with a Zouave in the foreground, the famous military painter has made a complete composition—not merely a study of a single figure.   The Zouave, solidly "planted" and leaning on his gun, is painted with all the strength and nervous force that characterize De Neuville's work, and in the background two officers are seen chatting, while a group of soldiers tend the camp fire.   The alert expression given by the attitude of the Zouave shows that he is a picket, and the setting of the scene in a forest with snow on the ground reveals the story of a small detachment of troops at an outpost in some winter campaign. Complete in every part, and with the attributes in drawing and color that belong to De Neuville's artistic achievement, this is a most satisfactory example of his work.

Height, 13¼ inches.   Width, 9¼ inches.
Signed at the left.   Dated 1878.

MADRAZO (RAYMUNDO DE).

No. 30. " Coco."

A white cockatoo on his tall perch, a light gray background, a couple of branches of japonica with scarlet blossoms, and three mice, two black and one white, nibbling seeds in the pan at the base of the perch, are the elements in this interesting picture. " Coco " wears an expression of refined curiosity with a pretense of indifference, and cocks his head on one side in a very taking way. As a piece of painting the picture is remarkable for the facility with which the feathers are rendered, the tender quality of the white, and the agreeable ensemble presented by the simple color harmony.

Height, 21½ inches. Width, 9 inches.
Signed at the right.

MUÑOZ (DOMINGO).

No. 31.   The Armorer.

Two guardsmen of the time of Louis XIII
(the epoch when d'Artagnan and the Three Mus-
keteers fought their battles and pursued their
exciting adventures), clad in buckskin doublets,
sashes, and plumed hats, are shown in this composition in an armorer's workshop. The armorer himself is seen taking down swords from
his shelves at the left of the canvas, to submit to
the inspection of his soldier customers. Both of
the guardsmen are evidently fighting men, and
are bronzed and hardy. In the back part of the
shop appears the forge, with a man nude to the
waist dimly seen at work before the fire. The
color scheme of the picture, with its chief tones
of gray, yellow, and black, and its telling notes
of red and crimson in the costumes and accessories, is a very distinguished one, and it is carried
out with fine artistic feeling. There is a great
deal of excellent detail painting, and the ensemble
is well preserved, making a work of decided personal quality and great beauty of general aspect.

Height, 11 inches.   Length, 14 inches.
Signed at the left.   Dated 1883.

MORGAN (WILLIAM).

Born in London in 1826. Pupil of the National Academy of Design, New York ; associate member of the Academy. He is a widely-known painter of genre and portraits, and many of his works are in private collections in the United States.

No. 32. " Born Tired."

This boy with his hands in his pockets, a straw hat on his head, and an expression both of face and figure that seems to indicate that he is content to be lazy, is painted with quiet humor. His gingham shirt and faded trousers proclaim him a product of village life ; his *ennui* proceeding, perhaps, as much from his dull surroundings as from any inherent disinclination to be active if something interested him sufficiently. The color is subdued, and the handling unobtrusive.

Height, 16 inches. Width, 10 inches.
Signed at the right.

MONCHABLON (F. JAN).

No. 33. "La Neige va tomber."

In this beautiful winter landscape a wide road leads from the front of the picture to a town lying in a valley. Along the top of the incline are houses, and in the hollow below a church spire. A carrier's cart is on its way to the town, and the tracks appear in the old snow on the roadway. Everything is wrapped in snow, the atmosphere is still, the sky dull gray, and, as expressed in the title, the snow is about to fall again. In so dreary a picture of winter as this, the artist has infused a fine poetic sentiment, and portrays the scene with the most delightful breadth and simplicity. The subtle values of the white snow at varying distances, the broad expanse of winter's mantle, and the exquisitely gradated sky—a never-failing point of excellence in Monchablon's work—are all given with fidelity and artistic unity.

Height, 15 inches. Length, 22 inches.
Signed at the right. Dated 1887.

JACQUE (CHARLES ÉMILE).

Born in Paris, May 23, 1813 ; died there in 1894. Celebrated for his pictures of sheep and poultry, and for his etchings. He was a Chevalier of the Legion of Honor, and received in addition to Salon medals, and other honors, a gold medal at the Paris Exposition of 1889. Few French artists have a more widely extended reputation, and his works are highly valued by collectors both in Europe and America.

No. 34. The Pasture.

On a sort of plateau with a field in the middle distance, and hills and the sky beyond, with the foliage of the spreading branches of a tree filling the upper part of the picture, sits a shepherdess tending her flock. A ewe and lamb appear in the foreground, and other sheep are seen to the right under the trees. The sheep are skillfully painted, of course—as Jacque is the painter—and the general tone of the canvas is rather light in color, without sombre notes. The peaceful sentiment of the subject is artistically interpreted, and the ensemble of the picture is harmonious and attractive.

Height, 18 inches. Width, 15 inches. Signed at the right.

MAX (GABRIEL).

Born in Prague, August 25, 1840. Son of the sculptor, Josef Max ; pupil of Prague Academy, Vienna Academy, and of Piloty of Munich. First exhibited in 1867, and is one of the most celebrated artists in the German School. Gold medals in Berlin and Munich. His " Last Token—Christian Martyr" is in the Wolfe Collection, Metropolitan Museum, New York.

No. 35. Marguerite.

A beautiful full type of maidenhood is shown in this head by the famous German painter. Its pale color but fleshy, texture, the blonde hair, brown eyes, white neck and shoulders, and the bit of bluish drapery over the bust, make a sympathetic, expressive picture. It is modelled with a full brush and the flesh tints are especially luminous. A characteristic example of the best work of an artist whose pictures are individual in style and always possess artistic qualities.

Height, 19 inches. Width, 15¼ inches.
Signed at the left.

JIMENEZ Y ARANDA (JOSÉ).

Born in Seville, Spain, 1832. Brother of Luis Jimenez and pupil of Seville Academy. Medals in Munich and Paris.

No. 36. The Old Notary.

Care and ability are shown in the painting of this figure of an elderly man in a flowered coat who is cutting a quill, and whose expression—with spectacles on nose—shows intentness and good humor tinctured with the dry-as-dust character of his avocation. The chair, table, inkstand, and other accessories are in character with the figure, and the picture shows conscientious, clever work throughout.

Height, 14 inches. Width, 10⅜ inches. Signed at the right. Dated 1889.

PILTZ (PROF. OTTO).

Genre and portrait painter of the Contemporary German School. His work is celebrated for its excellent study of character and good quality of color.

No. 37. Wide Awake.

A head of a jolly, flaxen-haired boy with big blue-gray eyes and a rosy, healthy complexion. The face is alert in expression and full of boyish character. It is skillfully and amply painted and especially notable for the fresh, strong quality of the color.

Height, 8 inches. Length, 10 inches. Signed at the upper left. Dated 1881.

GRISON (JULES ADOLPHE).

No. 38.   At the Antiquary's.

In this picture a beautifully painted figure of a man with powdered hair and wearing a Louis Quinze coat of red velvet, is seated with one hand holding a silver-topped long cane and the other holding out before him a little conch-like vase, forms the motive of the composition, while the dealer behind him—facing the spectator—leans over in an attitude of expectation.   The still-life in the picture is extremely well painted and the color scheme is most agreeable.   The eye rests with delight on the figure of the man in the chair ; for although the picture is one of great merit in every part, there is something about this personification that is rarely individual and striking.   It would be hard to find anywhere a more ably painted figure, and it, of itself, gives this excellent work an extraordinary interest.

Height, 9¼ inches.   Width, 7¼ inches.
Signed at the right.

MONCHABLON (F. JAN).

No 39.   Fa* (Aquarelle).

In this beautiful design we see Monchablon in a new light.   His decorative fancy is seen to be fertile and picturesque, and the water-color medium is handled with lightness of touch and sureness of effect.   On the right is a great beechwood tree, on the trunk of which a young peasant is cutting the name of his sweetheart, Marie, who also stands beside him.   At the left there is a stream with reeds and water plants reflected in its tranquil surface.   In color this piece is charming, the light tints producing an effect that is extremely pleasing.

Height, 12 inches.   Length, 24 inches.
Signed at the right.

DAUBIGNY (CHARLES FRANÇOIS).

Born in Paris, February 15, 1817; died there, February 20, 1878. Pupil of Edmé François Daubigny at first, then visited Italy, and on his return to Paris studied under Paul Delaroche. Exhibited constantly at the Salon from 1838 to the year of his death. Various medals, and Officer of the Legion of Honor. Ordinarily grouped with Corot and the Barbizon painters, and one of the greatest landscape painters that ever lived.

No. 40. On the Oise.

This composition shows one of the scenes which the great Daubigny loved to paint—a view on the river Oise, along which he used to float in his house-boat studio. A road at the left winds up the hill on the bank of the river, and some men are seen watering their horses, while women are washing clothes at the brink. In the middle of the picture some tall trees stand up against the sky of blue and white with dramatic effect, and the opposite bank is covered with trees. The fine general tone of this picture with its frank color in the sky and its subtle greens and grays in the landscape, make it a brilliant example of the famous painter.

Height, 18¼ inches. Length, 27½ inches. Signed at the left.

JACQUE (CHARLES ÉMILE).

No. 41. A Hot Summer Day.

A majestic picture, embracing the finest qualities of the great sheep and landscape painter. The foreground slopes upward and shows a few rocks, and old sod such as sheep delight to feed on. On the slope is a flock of sheep, their heads close together, cropping the short grass and herbage. In the middle of the composition rises a great tree with its widespread branches reaching to the top of the canvas. Behind it is another, and beyond is the edge of a forest. In the shade lies a young farmer in his shirt sleeves with his dog beside him. The white note made by the shirt, the black note made by the dog, appear in the color scheme with telling effect, and are balanced on the other side of the composition by two or three sheep with black or dark brown fleece. The trunk of the great tree is massive, and solidly and realistically painted ; the foliage is carefully studied and rendered with great breadth of handling and richness of color. The sky is gray, very fine and luminous in effect, and at the left of the picture is a plain with distant hills. The sunlight bathes the landscape in warm, golden light, and the splendid greens and browns and grays, appear in a matchless harmony of color. This is one of the most imposing and beautiful of the works of Jacque, and fully deserves the title of masterpiece.

Height, 29¼ inches. Width, 25¼ inches.
Signed at the right.

TROYON (CONSTANT).

Born at Sèvres, August 28, 1810; died in Paris, February 21, 1865. Pupil of Riocreux, Poupart, and Roqueplan. He visited Holland in 1847, and after 1848 introduced animals in his landscapes. The greatest cattle painter of the century, and one of the first landscape painters. Chevalier of the Legion of Honor, and received during his career many high artistic honors.

No. 42. The Woodchopper.

Troyon, as is well known, achieved great success as a landscape painter before he took up the study of animals. A fine example of his landscape work is " The Lane," sold this season in the Wm. H. Stewart collection. " The Woodchopper " is an equally remarkable picture. In the foreground is a felled tree at the roadside, with dead leaves clinging to its branches, and a man swinging his axe. A tall tree on the left, a plain, and a distant line of forest beyond compose the picture, with a fine sky over all, with banks of gray and white clouds. The blue shows in the spaces between the cloud masses, and the picture is notable for its distinguished scheme of color and virile painting. The warm tints of nature are interpreted with a fine reserve force, in no place inclining to hot browns or heaviness in the grays, and the general effect is imposing and restful. It is not unlike a Rousseau in general aspect, but contains its own distinctive character—the robust art of a painter whose work never fails to attract by its sincerity and strength.

Height, 19 inches. Width, 14 inches.
Signed at the right.

ROUSSEAU (PIERRE ÉTIENNE THÉODORE).

Born in Paris, April 15, 1812; died at Barbizon, December 22, 1867. Pupil of Rémond and of Lethière. With Corot, Daubigny, Dupré, and Diaz, he founded the modern French school of landscape painting. He was at first unsuccessful at the Salon, but his ability was afterward recognized, though not so fully as it should have been, owing to official intrigues. He was made a Chevalier of the Legion of Honor in 1852, but did not secure the coveted promotion to the grade of officer. Universally considered one of the great glories of French art.

No. 43. Ploughing in the Morning.

A delicious small work by the great landscape master of Barbizon. A field where a man is ploughing with a team of gray horses, with tall trees against the sky beyond. A blue sky suffused with morning mist and a few little clouds floating on high. In the distance a figure in red makes a telling note in the color scheme, and a white house is seen embowered among the trees. This is a most poetic little canvas, and in tenderness, atmosphere, and delicacy of color quite beyond compare. It is full, complete, and in every way satisfying and delightful.

Height, 6 inches. Length, 10 inches.
Signed at the right.

DIAZ DE LA PEÑA (NARCISO VIRGILIO).

Born at Bordeaux, of Spanish parents, August 28, 1808; died at Mentone, November 18, 1876. He began the study of art as a painter on porcelain, and afterward took up painting figures and landscape in oil. He became the friend and companion of Rousseau, Millet, Troyon, and other great French painters, and lived many years at Barbizon, painting landscapes of the Forest of Fontainebleau. Chevalier of the Legion of Honor. Universally admitted to be one of the great lights of the modern French School, and ranked in the highest class of landscape painters of the century.

No. 44.   Twilight in Fontainebleau Forest.

Known as "The Offenbach Diaz" and was painted by the artist for the composer, who was his intimate friend. Mr. Paul Detrimont wished to buy it, but not even after the composer's death could he secure it from his widow. He finally purchased it at the sale of Madame Offenbach's effects, and it was bought from him by Mr. Disbecker. The father of Mr. Paul Detrimont was the friend of Millet, Corot, Troyon, Diaz, and other famous painters, and his house was often made the place of their reunions in Paris. This small but very complete and beautiful panel shows a road leading up through a depression in the forest with dark trees in silhouette against a sky which is clouded with gray, with bits of blue appearing here and there and a mass of warm, white clouds at the horizon. A solitary horseman is introduced with dramatic effect in the roadway, and the last light of the day is concentrated on a bank of shale on the left of the composition, which contrasts with fine effect with the iron-gray of the clouds, the dark green of the trees, and the grays and cool dark browns in the foreground. The color scheme is distinguished and admirable in its unity, and the composition as a whole is remarkable for restrained force.

Height, 8¼ inches. Length, 13¼ inches.
Signed at the right.

RICHTER (GUSTAVE KARL LUDWIG).

Born in Berlin, August 31, 1823; died there August 23, 1884. Pupil of Berlin Academy, and, in Paris, of Léon Cogniet. Medals in Paris, Berlin, Brussels, Vienna, Munich, and Philadelphia. Received from the German Emperor the famous order *pour le merite*. His works, portraits, and genre, are in many public galleries in Europe.

No. 45. The Picture Book.

A minute but very complete genre picture, with six figures in a home-like interior, the whole no bigger than a man's head. A young girl with smoothly brushed hair and a lace collar is playing mother to a group of children gathered about her knees, to whom she is telling the stories connected with the pictures in the book she is showing them. The children wear quaint little costumes of the German village folk, and the expression of the faces and the attitudes of the figures show intentness and interest. The picture—the only cabinet-size genre subject by this artist known to be in America—is carefully finished, and in its unpretentious artistic rendering of a pretty scene in every-day life, recalls the Dutch masters, especially Terburg.

Height, 7 inches. Width, 6½ inches. Signed at the left. Dated 1852.

GRISON (JULES ADOLPHE).

No. 46. The Rendezvous.

This is a perfect gem of painting. A cavalier with a red coat on a black horse is waiting at the door in a garden wall, and steed and rider show an attitude of expectation. The cavalier with his powdered hair and long, riding boots, the saddle cloth of blue and gold, the bridle and trappings, are painted in minute perfection. The horse is finely drawn and his silky coat shines in the sun. Over the wall the trees in a park are seen and the shadow of the horse falls on the ground near the gate. Every detail is rendered in a manner that would do credit to Meissonier, and there is a fullness and breadth about the tiny panel that is as pleasing as it is wonderful. The picture may be carefully studied and close examination will reveal a hundred charming bits of work and all united in a harmonious whole.

Height, 5¼ inches. Width, 4¼ inches.
Signed at the right.

LELOIR (MAURICE).

Born in Paris, November 1, 1853. Pupil of his father, J. B. A. Leloir, and of his brother, Louis Leloir. Medal at the Salon of 1878. As well as having a high reputation as a genre painter of exquisite fancy, he is known as one of the cleverest illustrators of the time. His drawings in water color for an edition de luxe of Sterne's *Sentimental Journey* are considered to be among the finest productions of our time in this branch of art.

No. 47. French Fair.

The talented and *spirituel* painter of French gayety in the best sense of the word here gives us a scene in the outdoor amusements of the people. A tall hussar, in the red costume of a century ago, with his arms full of winnings at the shooting booths—a white rabbit, sheets of macaroons, a painted vase, and other trinkets—stops to talk to a pretty vendor of cakes and wine who has her wares for sale under a striped marquee. The fine, red note in the hussar's uniform is repeated in a more delicate tint in the sleeves of the young woman's bodice, and various gradations of red and white in other parts of the picture make up a scheme of color that is very pleasing. Beyond the cake-stand the tents and booths of the rest of the fair, with people in groups and walking about, and the green sward and foliage complete the setting for this charming *fête champêtre*. Technically, the picture is extremely clever, and while in the whole work the treatment is light-handed and deft, it also gives evidence of that sobriety of handling, and of that honesty of method, which have gained for French modern genre such high consideration.

Height, 12 inches.   Length, 16 inches.
Signed at the right.   Dated 1877.

MONCHABLON (F. JAN).

No. 48.   Un Coin de Chatillon.

At the foot of a road leading down hill into the picture, the town of Chatillon lies embowered among the trees. A church spire rises up at the right and there is a red-roofed cottage at the bend of the road. Beyond is a broad expanse of country with hills and plains, and over all a summer sky of blue with small white clouds here and there. Possesses the characteristics of the artist, and is an interesting picture both in subject and treatment.

Signed at the right.   Dated 1889.

PASINI (ALBERTO).

Born at Busseto, near Parma. Contemporary painter. Pupil of Eugène Ciceri, Isabey, and Rousseau. Medal of Honor at the Paris Universal Exposition, 1878; Officer of the Legion of Honor. One of the most distinguished of the Oriental painters of modern times, whose pictures enjoy a widespread popularity, and are esteemed by artists for their remarkable technical qualities.

No. 49. Market Scene, Constantinople.

Here are the picturesque architecture of the Bosphorus beautifully painted, the deep blue sky, the brilliant light, and the transparent shadows. In the foreground are people standing in groups, seated in crowds, or wandering about horses, a dog asleep in the sun, and jars, fruits, vegetables, and many other things. There is a wealth of color, but all is held together in a consistent whole. These market scenes are a favorite subject with this celebrated painter, but it is not often that one sees a picture by him with so much animation. Mr. Disbecker told the artist he wanted the picture with plenty of life, and he got it. It is a most characteristic and perfect Pasini, and has in addition this feature of being full of life and movement.

Height, 12½ inches. Length, 16½ inches. Signed at the right. Dated 1882.

GRISON (JULES ADOLPHE).

No. 50. The New Coat.

A very interesting genre picture, with a vein of humor in the subject. Monsieur and Madame, who are fine "county people," have brought the boy they have adopted to the provincial tailor to have new clothes tried on which are to fittingly dress him for his new life. The costumes are of the time of the Directory. The fair-haired boy stands at the left with his arms held straight downward and the palms of the hands and fingers rigidly stretched out, while the old tailor, looking over his spectacles, seems to say to his aristocratic patrons : " Never fear, I will fix everything just as it should be." The lady, wearing a gown of narrow-striped stuff, and the master, in a coat of rich brown, standing beside her, look on the scene with interest in their faces, and behind the counter the old tailor's wife, in a white cap and big linen frill, holds the shop cat in her arms. A bird in its cage is suspended from the ceiling, and a number of other accessories are introduced, making an appropriate setting for the figures. The composition is excellent and tells the story admirably. The general effect of color in the picture is quiet, but very agreeable and effective. Everything is painted in a direct, frank manner, and with full understanding of the exigencies of the subject. A fine specimen of the best school of modern French genre.

Height, 18 inches. Length, 21½ inches.
Signed at the right.

MONCHABLON (F. JAN).

No. 51. Pasturage au Soleil.

Marvellously brilliant effects of sunlight. In the meadow in the foreground are a man and woman and some cows which are perfectly painted, and in the middle distance are some houses nestled among the trees. On a hill to the left is a town with roofs and spires, and distant hills beyond are crowned with trees. This picture is simply wonderful in its veracious transcription of nature and its dazzling rendering of the full light of the sun. It is nature itself, and marks its painter as an artist of the highest rank in the depiction of landscape.

Height, 18½ inches. Length, 26 inches.
Signed at the left.

ISRAELS (JOZEF).

Born at Gröningen in 1824, and was a pupil in
Amsterdam of Cornelis Kruseman. Afterward
studied in Paris with Picot. Resides at The Hague.
Officer of the Legion of Honor and Knight of the
Order of Leopold. Formerly painted historical
subjects, but has achieved his wide reputation as a
painter of Dutch genre.

No. 52. Dutch Interior.

This is one of the best examples of the work
of Holland's famous painter of figures indoors
and domestic scenes, and belongs to his very best
period. It shows none of the ropy handling
noticeable in his latest work and none of the mud-
diness of color. Rarely is a picture by Israels
seen in this country now—unless it be in some
fine private collection—that shows as well as this
the meritorious character of his art, both in sentiment and in color quality. At one side of a
table, before a wide window, with muslin curtains, looking out upon a garden and trees, an
old woman is seated with her knitting in her lap.
She has stopped her work to look at the house cat
lapping milk in an earthen bowl placed on the
floor. On the table is a tray with dishes, tea-pot,
and other articles. The general tone of the picture is warm and glowing, but with no trace of
" foxiness "; the grays, yellows, pale greens,
blacks and dark blues, are full and resonant.

There are quality, strength, and virility in the painting, and the composition is simple and effective.

Height, 20 inches. Length, 28 inches.
Signed at the left.

DUPRÉ (JULIEN).

No. 53. The Haymakers' Lunch.

Three figures in a charming Normandy landscape. One peasant girl in blue with dark red 'kerchief on her head is standing up while she cuts a huge loaf of pain de ménage ; another girl with a black bodice, white underwaist, and white skirt with large buff apron, is sitting on the bunches of hay piled up at the right of the picture. An old man in a blue blouse reclines behind them with his pipe in his mouth. The girl in white and black pours out cider from a bottle, and there is a big basket beside her that contains the rest of the lunch. It is a bright summer day and clouds of white float in the sky, casting shadows on the fields. The sky is fine in color, and the tone of the hay-field with its stacks is tender and truthful. An important example of the work of a deservedly popular artist.

Height, 26 inches. Length, 32 inches.
Signed at the left. Dated 1886.

LAUGÉE (GEORGES).

No. 54. Visit to the Fields.

Rich sunset effect. On the outskirts of a French village, where a man is digging up potatoes in a field, his wife has come with her baby on her arm and her basket to see how the work comes on. The town with its cottage roofs and church spire among the trees comes out in dark relief against the glowing sky of red and orange. The entire picture is illumined by the warm glow of the setting sun, and the gray clouds in the upper part of the sky form an effective contrast to the brilliant tints at the horizon.

Height, 26 inches. Length, 32 inches. Signed at the right. Dated 1887.

MULLER (CHARLES-LOUIS).

Born in Paris, December 22, 1815; died there within the last decade. Pupil of Baron Gros and Léon Cogniet and of the École des Beaux-Arts. He was a Member of the Institute and Officer of the Legion of Honor; artistic director of the manufacture of the Gobelin tapestries from 1850 to 1853. His "Charlotte Corday, in Prison," is in the Corcoran Gallery, Washington.

No. 55. The May Queen.

This charming picture is by the painter of the celebrated "Roll-Call of Last Victims of the Reign of Terror," which was long one of the great attractions of the Luxembourg Museum in Paris, and belongs to the French Government. The "May Queen" is a pretty girl painted life-size in three-quarter length, costumed in a V-shaped corsage of pale blue and a white skirt with a tulle scarf around her neck, blue ribbons on her sleeves, and white mitts on her hands. She is delightful in her simplicity and grace, and her dark hair falls in ringlets on her forehead and behind her ears. With a charmingly suggested movement she holds out lightly the skirt of her gown with the finger tips of both hands, and on either side of her are green leaves and spring foliage. The head is suavely modelled and is limpid in color, and the general effect of the whole figure is engaging in its innocent and budding youthfulness.

Height, 44 inches.   Width, 31 inches.
Signed at the left.

WAGNER (FERDINAND).

No. 56. The Shrine by the Wayside.

A well-known composition which has been engraved, and has long been a popular picture. A young and pretty girl in a Marguerite costume kneels before a shrine on a massive pillar of stone entwined with vines and foliage. Her head is seen in profile, and is comely in its simple grace. She holds a long garland of field flowers, all very carefully painted, and the upper part of the figure is relieved against a sunset sky. A field of ripe wheat occupies the middle of the picture, and a tree grows up by the side of the shrine. A notable example of effective figure-painting in a composition with a single figure, and remarkable for its rich color effect.

Height, 44 inches. Width, 29¼ inches.

Signed at the left.

MONCHABLON (F. JAN).

No. 57. Les Patureaux.

A wide meadow, with a tranquil stream flowing through it between deep banks, cattle and sheep grazing, two peasant girls in gray woollens in the foreground tending the flocks, and some boys making a fire of sticks in another part of the meadow, are the principal features of this splendid picture, which was exhibited at the Salon of 1888, and attracted great attention. It is late afternoon on a September day, and the whole picture is in shadow—very luminous atmospheric shadow—except where some distant hills catch the dying rays of the sun. The sky is pale and full of light, with a few pinkish lilac clouds at the horizon and a little white fleck floating on high. The picture is full of detail, as all of Monchablon's works are, and everything is rendered with unerring fidelity. Frankly and broadly painted, delicate but virile in color, luminous and atmospheric, with its sky of exquisitely gradated values, this important work must be rated among the most remarkable of modern landscapes.

Height, 36 inches. Length, 50 inches.
Signed at the right. Dated 1887.

AMERICAN ART ASSOCIATION,
MANAGERS.

THOMAS E. KIRBY,
Auctioneer.